COMPTIA NETWORK+ IN 21 DAYS
N10-006 Q & A Study Guide

By: C.V.Conner

Comptia Network+ in 21 Days N10-006 Study Guide by C.V.Conner, Ph.D.
© 2016 by C.V.Conner. All rights reserved.

No part of this book may be reproduced in any written, electronic, recording, or photocopying without written permission of the publisher or author. The exception would be in the case of brief quotations embodied in the critical articles or reviews and pages where permission is specifically granted by the publisher or author.

Although every precaution has been taken to verify the accuracy of the information contained herein, the author and publisher assume no responsibility for any errors or omissions. No liability is assumed for damages that may result from the use of information contained within.

Books may be purchased by contacting the publisher and author Email: sales@newdaypublishing.com

Cover Design: New Day Graphics, Inc.
Interior Design: New Day Publishing, LLC.
Publisher: New Day Publishing Company
Editor: Shara Editing Services
Creative Consultants: The Scott Day Group
Library of Congress Catalog Number:
ISBN: 978-1-365-30420-0
1. Computers 2. Internet 3. Certification 4. Technology
First Edition
Printed in the United States of America

Introduction

Let's face it, we all know people who are irrational when it comes to getting a better education and providing for their families. No matter how hard you try to reason with them, it never works because they insist that they need thousands of dollars to return to college, or that their present position in life will not allow them to get a better education. So what's the solution? How do you explain to them that a good home study program can completely take the place of a traditional college campus? What can you do to make those people understand that computer technology is a great career field, and that getting into the field can be as easy as 1, 2, 3, all from the comforts of your own home?

In his book, *Comptia A+ For Newbies*, C.V.Conner shared his bestselling formula for breaking into the computer field through his own and other highly proven home study programs. Now, in his breakthrough new 21 days series, he brings his certification magic to the most difficult group of all—the downright traditional college focused.

As a information technology professional, Conner has seen his share of traditional college graduates entering the IT field and he knows from experience that you can't simply graduate with enough experience and knowledge to pass the certification exams. The key to handling these exams is have the exact questions, answers, and in some cases the explanations that you can expect to see on the actual exams! That radically changes the playing field and transforms you from being just a graduate technician into a successfully certified computer professional. Comptia Network+ in 21 Days N10-006 Study Guide provides you with more than enough questions, answers, and explanations where needed, and covers:

The configuration, management, and troubleshooting of both common and wireless networks as you will see on the actual exam.

You can't reason your way to computer certifications—but you can gain them quickly. This powerful and practical study guide shows you how.

Throughout this guide, Conner has tried to use uniform typographical conventions. Hopefully they aid readability.

Trademarks Mentioned:

Throughout this and all other technology books written by this author, the use of multiple trademark names and/or slogans is mentioned. It is permitted and we use the Trademarks in relation to products and/or documentation owned by the respective trademark owners, and we do not use any trademark name and/slogan in any manner which is confusing or misleading; or causes confusion or misleads as to any affiliation or endorsement of our books.

Microsoft, Windows, Windows NT, Windows 2000, and Windows XP are trademarks and/or registered trademarks of Microsoft Corporation.
Red Hat is a trademark of Red Hat, Inc., in the United States and other countries.
SuSE is a trademark of Novell.
Linux is a registered trademark of Linus Torvalds.
UNIX is a registered trademark in the United States and other countries, licensed exclusively through X/Open Company Ltd.
GNU is a registered trademark of the Free Software Foundation.
Other product names mentioned herein may be trademarks and/or registered trademarks of their respective companies

About This Study Guide

You're reading Comptia Network+ in 21 Days N10-006 Study Guide, first published in August 2016 by New Day Publishing Company.

We've released this #1 study guide for a couple of reasons. First, we love Comptia Network+ and we want the certification to be as accessible as possible. Many technicians have been blessed to attend a traditional college and learn their craft from well-received local teachers. But far more people have found themselves having to start a new career, many already carrying the burden of unemployment while trying to raise their families. We set out to create a top-notch guide for the latter, and we wanted to release a product that could be successfully completed from the comforts of your own home, all on your own schedule.

Second, it turns out that writing books technology is fundamentally difficult: our words are often outdated before the book even reaches the printer. But by releasing this type Q & A study guides, however, "the ink is never dry" — we are afforded the opportunity to revise and update each edition as the exam changes!

Note: *For obvious reasons there are no interactive sims included within this book. But for the sake of preparedness we ask that you go thru the motions using a separate sheet of paper for your answers, and when you feel you have completed your choices move to the next.*

Acknowledgements

The most gratifying aspect of working on our new Comptia series of books and study guides is the community. We've been especially lucky that this series has attracted a smart, motivated, and friendly bunch of people anxious to enter the IT field. Your positive reviews and comments are indispensable and we'd like to thank each and every one of you. We're especially grateful for your purchase of this series and for you taking the time to review the book in depth and leave us your helpful positive comments.

Many thanks to our creative consultants, The Scott Day Group. Without Scott this book would be too littered with errors, inaccuracies, and broken names to read. We feel very lucky that someone as talented as Scott found the time to help us out.

We're also grateful for all the hard work the people at New Day put into this book. They've been amazingly supportive and patient; this book wouldn't have come together without a lot of work on their part.

Finally, of course, thanks to our friends, families, and associates who've graciously tolerated our mental absence while we finished this work.

About the Author

Dr. C.V.Conner is an Information Technology expert with premier certifications of multiply vendors including MCSE, MCDBA, and MCSA. He's known in IT Certification circles as one of the pioneers of "Quic-Pass" brain dumps", and in technical circles as "the guy who invented The 21 Days Approach."

He was lead developer of the best selling "MCSE in 21 Days", and helped launch the release into global distribution
Dr. Conner lives in Houston, USA.

Let's Get Started

"In the beginning, this file was without form, and void; and emptiness was upon it's face. And the Fingers of the Author moved upon the face of the keyboard. And the Author said, Let there be words, and there were words."

The Comptia Network+ in 21 Days N10-006 Study Guide, describes or lays out the exact questions, answers, and in some cases, the explainations you should expect to know to pass the N10-006 exam. It is intended for people who know next to nothing about what it's going to take to pass this exam, but who have already mastered at least the basics of Comptia Network+. This study guide doesn't give you all the background and reasons for the questions on the actual exam; that is described in our same titled Training Manual.

The structure of this study guide is such that many of the questions and answers will be seen in different wording, so you can be prepared for any trick questions come actual exam day. However, this study guide is first and foremost a tutorial and can be read sequentially or as a whole.
This study guide is intended to be used completely independently. If you have studied our training manual of this same title, there is absolutely nothing else that you need to pass your exam. But even if you have hands-on knowledge and/or have chosen to complete a traditional college course for Network+, we hope that you will use this study guide alone to actually pass your exam.

There is no 1 best N10-006 study guide, different authors have different sets of advice and many people have a setup they have built up themselves. This book is not targeted at downgrading any one author. Authors can and do vary considerably. However, in trying to get you past this exam quickly and easily, rather than just piling up on all the information that possibly connects to any one test question we take into consideration there is much information that is not necessary to answer the question correctly. Reading everything will, naturally, increase your understanding of the job and should make using and administering in the field more productive. But that is not necessarily the case in testing. "Less Is More".

Understanding is the key to success with exams. This manual could just provide hours of explanations, but what would you do when confronted by a trick question? If the book can provide correct questions and answers that you could simply memorize, then extended explanations are not required. The answers will be self evident.

One particular point where corners have been cut in this and all of our upcoming technology study guides is that many things that are already well documented in our training are not always covered here because they are not covered on the exam(s). Only the questions and answers and as much explanation as is necessary for passing the exam is presented.

Like all of my writing, this book has been developed for newbies, although it will cover some of the most advanced and important topics. What that means is that I have taken as much of the technical and advanced topics as possible and broken them down into kind of a plain Jane-simple English format so that you can easily grasp the technology and skills that will be needed to pass your exam here.

Now, a question I get a lot when I release a new book for newbies is can you take my simple study guide and pass an exam on the subject? And the answer is always the same "You bet you can! But, at the same time, I do not recommend that you go out and apply for a Network Administrator position just because you passed the exam. Why not? Simple. There's usually a lot of information that goes into any technology book and you will need to know a great deal of that information to go out and enter the workforce. So I always recommend that you commit yourself to a quality Home, Self-Study, or Traditional training program before taking any certification exam if you want to be able to perform at a high level in the field. My training books are always written to do that for you in the shortest time possible.

Also, let me give you my big disclaimer for this book before we get started, and make sure you understand this. I include this now in most all of my study guides and training books because it's very important for you. First of all, batteries are not included. That means you cannot just sit and read the information while you're half drifting off into la la land and just kind of let eight and half, nine hours of information blow by and think that you're going to really know this stuff. You will have to energize yourself. You will have to grab onto the information and memorize the data. Just understand just memorizing a small percentage of the data from this book alone probably will get you that passing grade on the actual exam, but you will not have enough understanding to do the job in the real world. So you need to have at least a basic understanding of all the topics and technologies before you enter the work force. That is not to say that you need to know everything, but you do need to know enough to be able to perform many administrative needs without needing a second head standing over you for 8 hours.

I'm going to give you all the questions and answers in this book, everything you need to know to pass the exam. But in terms of expectations, lifelong learning is critical. Understand then that certified, experienced or not, 99% of all employers is going to give you some form of OJT (On the Job Training) before you're allowed or trusted to barge into these really high-tech areas. So stop worrying about a need for traditional classroom courses.

Everything you need to take that huge step up the IT ladder is in your hands right now! But preparing for a career in the computer field presents many people with several challenges. Yet those who have a made-up mind to continually study and learn, and stick to it will more often than not perform better than those people who just wing it. I always say that most people don't plan to fail, they simply fail because they didn't plan at all. I pride myself on having an ability to see the things that are off a little bit in other's studying or learning methods. I am by no means the smartest guy on the block, but I am a leading test taker and career maker in information technology. And the very best tip I can give you on advancing your career in information technology is to be coachable. Allowing me to coach you doesn't make me any smarter than you. In fact, great coaching is nothing more than helping people discover what they already know. So if you want to maximize your potential in anything, be coachable my friend.

Understand that human beings are emotional creatures and all competent coaches are experts at stoking the fires that already burn within them. As your coach, I can't create a flame, but I'm very good at turning a small flame into a blow torch. That means that just the small flame that led you to buy this book is the only prerequisite for your greatness. Whatever you do, don't accept average. Average people will only accept the amount of coaching their egos will allow. But all great champions are well known for being the most open to coaching. The bigger the champion, the more open-minded they are. Just think about it.

You must make up in your mind right now to care nothing about ego satisfaction when it comes to improving your results -- all you need to look for is an edge, no matter how slight. The logic behind this is simple: 99.99 % of the times, the only thing that favors a winner is a slight edge in thinking, strategy or technique. Average people tend to view the thoughts and ideas of others not only as potentially useful, but also as threatening to their egos and existence. As a result, most are severely limited in the size and scope of their accomplishments. So I beg you, don't spend a substantial amount of time negotiating the price of victory. Become one with the mindset of "Whatever it takes".

Vendor: CompTIA

Exam Code: N10-006

Exam Name: CompTIA Network+ N10-006 Certification Exam

Question 1 -- Question

CompTIA N10-006
Network+ Certification Exam
Topic 1, Network Architecture

Q1
A technician has verified that a recent loss of network connectivity to multiple workstations is due to a bad CAT5 cable in the server room wall. Which of the following tools can be used to locate its physical location within the wall?
A. Cable certifier
B. Multimeter
C. Cable tester
D. Toner probe
Answer: D
Explanation:

Q2
Which of the following is used to authenticate remote workers who connect from offsite? (Select TWO).
A. OSPF
B. VTP trunking
C. Virtual PBX
D. RADIUS
E. 802.1x
Answer: D,E
Explanation:

Q3
Which of the following network infrastructure implementations would be used to support files being transferred between Bluetooth-enabled smartphones?
A. PAN
B. LAN
C. WLAN
D. MAN
Answer: A
Explanation:

Q4
Which of the following would be used in an IP-based video conferencing deployment? (Select TWO).
A. RS-232
B. 56k modem
C. Bluetooth
D. Codec
E. SIP
Answer: D,E
Explanation:

Q5
Which of the following helps prevent routing loops?
A. Routing table
B. Default gateway
C. Route summarization
D. Split horizon
Answer: D
Explanation:

Q6
Which of the following is MOST likely to use an RJ-11 connector to connect a computer to an ISP using a POTS line?
A. Multilayer switch
B. Access point
C. Analog modem
D. DOCSIS modem
Answer: C
Explanation:

Q7
An administrator has a virtualization environment that includes a vSAN and iSCSI switching. Which of the following actions could the administrator take to improve the performance of data transfers over iSCSI switches?
A. The administrator should configure the switch ports to auto-negotiate the proper Ethernet
settings.
B. The administrator should configure each vSAN participant to have its own VLAN.
C. The administrator should connect the iSCSI switches to each other over inter-switch links (ISL).
D. The administrator should set the MTU to 9000 on the each of the participants in the vSAN.
Answer: D
Explanation:

Q8
A network topology that utilizes a central device with point-to-point connections to all other devices is which of the following?
A. Star
B. Ring
C. Mesh
D. Bus
Answer: A
Explanation:

Q9
A technician is connecting a NAS device to an Ethernet network. Which of the following technologies will be used to encapsulate the frames?
A. HTTPS
B. Fibre channel
C. iSCSI
D. MS-CHAP
Answer: C
Explanation:

Q10
The network install is failing redundancy testing at the MDF. The traffic being transported is a mixture of multicast and unicast signals. Which of the

following would BEST handle the rerouting caused by the disruption of service?
A. Layer 3 switch
B. Proxy server
C. Layer 2 switch
D. Smart hub
Answer: A
Explanation:
Q11
A company wants to create highly available datacenters. Which of the following will allow the company to continue to maintain an Internet presence at all sites in the event that a WAN circuit at one site goes down?
A. Load balancer
B. VRRP
C. OSPF
D. BGP
Answer: D
Explanation:
Q12
A training class is being held in an auditorium. Hard-wired connections are required for all laptops that will be used. The network technician must add a switch to the room through which the laptops will connect for full network access. Which of the following must the technician configure on a switch port, for both switches, in order to create this setup?
A. DHCP
B. Split horizon
C. CIDR
D. TRUNK
Answer: D
Explanation:
Q13
Which of the following communication technologies would MOST likely be used to increase bandwidth over an existing fiber optic network by combining multiple signals at different wavelengths?
A. DWDM
B. SONET
C. ADSL
D. LACP
Answer: A
Explanation:

Q14
Which of the following WAN technologies is associated with high latency?
A. T1
B. Satellite
C. Cable
D. OCx
Answer: B
Explanation:
Q15
Which of the following provides accounting, authorization, and authentication via a centralized privileged database, as well as, challenge/response and password encryption?
A. Multifactor authentication
B. ISAKMP
C. TACACS+
D. Network access control
Answer: C
Explanation:
Q16
Which of the following is used to define how much bandwidth can be used by various protocols on the network?
A. Traffic shaping
B. High availability
C. Load balancing
D. Fault tolerance
Answer: A
Explanation:
Q17
Which of the following network topologies has a central, single point of failure?
A. Ring
B. Star
C. Hybrid
D. Mesh
Answer: B
Explanation:
Q18
A technician is helping a SOHO determine where to install the server. Which of the following should be considered FIRST?
A. Compatibility requirements

B. Environment limitations
C. Cable length
D. Equipment limitations
Answer: B
Explanation:

Q19
When convergence on a routed network occurs, which of the following is true?
A. All routers are using hop count as the metric
B. All routers have the same routing table
C. All routers learn the route to all connected networks
D. All routers use route summarization
Answer: C
Explanation:

Q20
A technician has been given a list of requirements for a LAN in an older building using CAT6 cabling. Which of the following environmental conditions should be considered when deciding whether or not to use plenum-rated cables?
A. Workstation models
B. Window placement
C. Floor composition
D. Ceiling airflow condition
Answer: D
Explanation:

Q21
A company has a new offering to provide access to their product from a central location rather than clients internally hosting the product on the client network. The product contains sensitive corporate information that should not be accessible from one client to another. This is an example of which of the following?
A. Public SaaS
B. Private SaaS
C. Hybrid IaaS
D. Community IaaS
Answer: B
Explanation:

Q22
Which of the following refers to a network that spans several buildings that are within walking distance of each other?

A. CAN
B. WAN
C. PAN
D. MAN
Answer: A
Explanation:
Q23
An administrator notices an unused cable behind a cabinet that is terminated with a DB-9 connector. Which of the following protocols was MOST likely used on this cable?
A. RS-232
B. 802.3
C. ATM
D. Token ring
Answer: A
Explanation:
Q24
Which of the following describes an IPv6 address of ::1?
A. Broadcast
B. Loopback
C. Classless
D. Multicast
Answer: B
Explanation:
Q25
A SQL server needs several terabytes of disk space available to do an uncompressed backup of a database. Which of the following devices would be the MOST cost efficient to use for this backup?
A. iSCSI SAN
B. FCoE SAN
C. NAS
D. USB flash drive
Answer: C
Explanation:
Q26
A technician needs to set aside addresses in a DHCP pool so that certain servers always receive the same address. Which of the following should be configured?
A. Leases
B. Helper addresses

C. Scopes
D. Reservations
Answer: D
Explanation:
Q27
Which of the following network elements enables unified communication devices to connect to and traverse traffic onto the PSTN?
A. Access switch
B. UC gateway
C. UC server
D. Edge router
Answer: B
Explanation:
Topic 2, Network Operations
Q28
A network technician receives the following alert from a network device: "High utilizations threshold exceeded on gi1/0/24 : current value 9413587.54" Which of the following is being monitored to trigger the alarm?
A. Speed and duplex mismatch
B. Wireless channel utilization
C. Network device CPU
D. Network device memory
E. Interface link status
Answer: E
Explanation:
Q29
A technician is configuring a managed switch and needs to enable 802.3af. Which of the following should the technician enable?
A. PoE
B. Port bonding
C. VLAN
D. Trunking
Answer: A
Explanation:
Q30
Which of the following protocols must be implemented in order for two switches to share VLAN information?
A. VTP
B. MPLS
C. STP

D. PPTP
Answer: A
Explanation:

Q31
After a recent breach, the security technician decides the company needs to analyze and aggregate its security logs. Which of the following systems should be used?
A. Event log
B. Syslog
C. SIEM
D. SNMP
Answer: C
Explanation:

Q32
A network technician is diligent about maintaining all system servers' at the most current service pack level available. After performing upgrades, users experience issues with server-based applications. Which of the following should be used to prevent issues in the future?
A. Configure an automated patching server
B. Virtualize the servers and take daily snapshots
C. Configure a honeypot for application testing
D. Configure a test lab for updates
Answer: D
Explanation:

Q33
A company has implemented the capability to send all log files to a central location by utilizing an encrypted channel. The log files are sent to this location in order to be reviewed. A recent exploit has caused the company's encryption to become unsecure. Which of the following would be required to resolve the exploit?
A. Utilize a FTP service
B. Install recommended updates
C. Send all log files through SMTP
D. Configure the firewall to block port 22
Answer: B
Explanation:

Q34
The RAID controller on a server failed and was replaced with a different brand. Which of the following will be needed after the server has been rebuilt and joined to the domain?

A. Vendor documentation
B. Recent backups
C. Physical IP address
D. Physical network diagram
Answer: B
Explanation:

Q35
A network technician has been tasked with designing a WLAN for a small office. One of the requirements of this design is that it is capable of supporting HD video streaming to multiple devices. Which of the following would be the appropriate wireless technology for this design?
A. 802.11g
B. 802.11ac
C. 802.11b
D. 802.11a
Answer: B
Explanation:

Q36
A company is experiencing accessibility issues reaching services on a cloud-based system. Which of the following monitoring tools should be used to locate possible outages?
A. Network analyzer
B. Packet analyzer
C. Protocol analyzer
D. Network sniffer
Answer: A
Explanation:

Q37
A company is experiencing very slow network speeds of 54Mbps. A technician has been hired to perform an assessment on the existing wireless network. The technician has recommended an 802.11n network infrastructure. Which of the following allows 802.11n to reach higher speeds?
A. MU-MIMO
B. LWAPP
C. PoE
D. MIMO
Answer: D
Explanation:

Q38

It has been determined by network operations that there is a severe bottleneck on the company's mesh topology network. The field technician has chosen to use log management and found that one router is making routing decisions slower than others on the network. This is an example of which of the following?
A. Network device power issues
B. Network device CPU issues
C. Storage area network issues
D. Delayed responses from RADIUS
Answer: B
Explanation:
Q39
After a company rolls out software updates, Ann, a lab researcher, is no longer able to use lab equipment connected to her PC. The technician contacts the vendor and determines there is an incompatibility with the latest IO drivers. Which of the following should the technician perform so that Ann can get back to work as quickly as possible?
A. Reformat and install the compatible drivers.
B. Reset Ann's equipment configuration from a backup.
C. Downgrade the PC to a working patch level.
D. Restore Ann's PC to the last known good configuration.
E. Roll back the drivers to the previous version.
Answer: E
Explanation:
Q40
A system administrator has been tasked to ensure that the software team is not affecting the production software when developing enhancements. The software that is being updated is on a very short SDLC and enhancements must be developed rapidly. These enhancements must be approved before being deployed. Which of the following will mitigate production outages before the enhancements are deployed?
A. Implement an environment to test the enhancements.
B. Implement ACLs that only allow management access to the enhancements.
C. Deploy an IPS on the production network.
D. Move the software team's workstations to the DMZ.
Answer: A
Explanation:
Q41

An administrator reassigns a laptop to a different user in the company. Upon delivering the laptop to the new user, the administrator documents the new location, the user of the device and when the device was reassigned. Which of the following BEST describes these actions?
A. Network map
B. Asset management
C. Change management
D. Baselines
Answer: B
Explanation:
Q42
Company policies require that all network infrastructure devices send system level information to a centralized server. Which of the following should be implemented to ensure the network administrator can review device error information from one central location?
A. TACACS+ server
B. Single sign-on
C. SYSLOG server
D. Wi-Fi analyzer
Answer: C
Explanation:
Q43
A network technician has been tasked to configure a new network monitoring tool that will examine interface settings throughout various network devices. Which of the following would need to be configured on each network device to provide that information in a secure manner?
A. S/MIME
B. SYSLOG
C. PGP
D. SNMPv3
E. RSH
Answer: D
Explanation:
Q44
Which of the following would be the result of a user physically unplugging a VoIP phone and connecting it into another interface with switch port security enabled as the default setting?
A. The VoIP phone would request a new phone number from the unified communications server.

B. The VoIP phone would cause the switch interface, that the user plugged into, to shutdown.
C. The VoIP phone would be able to receive incoming calls but will not be able to make outgoing calls.
D. The VoIP phone would request a different configuration from the unified communications server.
Answer: B
Explanation:

Q45
A company is deploying a new wireless network and requires 800Mbps network throughput. Which of the following is the MINIMUM configuration that would meet this need?
A. 802.11ac with 2 spatial streams and an 80MHz bandwidth
B. 802.11ac with 3 spatial streams and a 20MHz bandwidth
C. 802.11ac with 3 spatial streams and a 40MHz bandwidth
D. 802.11ac with 4 spatial streams and a 160MHz bandwidth
Answer: A
Explanation:

Q46
A technician would like to track the improvement of the network infrastructure after upgrades. Which of the following should the technician implement to have an accurate comparison?
A. Regression test
B. Speed test
C. Baseline
D. Statement of work
Answer: C
Explanation:

Q47
When two or more links need to pass traffic as if they were one physical link, which of the following would be used to satisfy the requirement?
A. Port mirroring
B. 802.1w
C. LACP
D. VTP
Answer: C
Explanation:

Q48
A VLAN with a gateway offers no security without the addition of:
A. An ACL.

B. 802.1w.
C. A RADIUS server.
D. 802.1d.
Answer: A
Explanation:
Q49
Network segmentation provides which of the following benefits?
A. Security through isolation
B. Link aggregation
C. Packet flooding through all ports
D. High availability through redundancy
Answer: A
Explanation:
Q50
A network technician must create a wireless link between two buildings in an office park utilizing the 802.11ac standard. The antenna chosen must have a small physical footprint and minimal weight as it will be mounted on the outside of the building. Which of the following antenna types is BEST suited for this solution?
A. Yagi
B. Omni-directional
C. Parabolic
D. Patch
Answer: A
Explanation:
Q51
The administrator's network has OSPF for the internal routing protocol. One port going out to the Internet is congested. The data is going out to the Internet, but queues up before sending. Which of the following would resolve this issue?
Output:
Fast Ethernet 0 is up, line protocol is up
Int ip address is 10.20.130.5/25
MTU 1500 bytes, BW10000 kbit, DLY 100 usec
Reliability 255/255, Tx load 1/255, Rx load 1/255
Encapsulation ospf, loopback not set
Keep alive 10
Half duplex, 100Mb/s, 100 Base Tx/Fx
Received 1052993 broadcasts
0 input errors

983881 packets output, 768588 bytes
0 output errors, 0 collisions, 0 resets
A. Set the loopback address
B. Change the IP address
C. Change the slash notation
D. Change duplex to full
Answer: D
Explanation:
Q52
An outside organization has completed a penetration test for a company. One of the items on the report is reflecting the ability to read SSL traffic from the web server. Which of the following is the MOST likely mitigation for this reported item?
A. Ensure patches are deployed
B. Install an IDS on the network
C. Configure the firewall to block traffic on port 443
D. Implement a VPN for employees
Answer: A
Explanation:
Q53
A system administrator wants to update a web-based application to the latest version. Which of the following procedures should the system administrator perform FIRST?
A. Remove all user accounts on the server
B. Isolate the server logically on the network
C. Block all HTTP traffic to the server
D. Install the software in a test environment
Answer: D
Explanation:
Q54
Multiple students within a networking lab are required to simultaneously access a single switch remotely. The administrator checks and confirms that the switch can be accessed using the console, but currently only one student can log in at a time. Which of the following should be done to correct this issue?
A. Increase installed memory and install a larger flash module.
B. Increase the number of VLANs configured on the switch.
C. Decrease the number of VLANs configured on the switch.
D. Increase the number of virtual terminals available.
Answer: D

Explanation:
Topic 3, Network Security
Q55
A technician needs to install software onto company laptops to protect local running services, from external threats. Which of the following should the technician install and configure on the laptops if the threat is network based?
A. A cloud-based antivirus system with a heuristic and signature based engine
B. A network based firewall which blocks all inbound communication
C. A host-based firewall which allows all outbound communication
D. A HIDS to inspect both inbound and outbound network communication
Answer: C
Explanation:
Q56
Which of the following physical security controls prevents an attacker from gaining access to a network closet?
A. CCTVs
B. Proximity readers
C. Motion sensors
D. IP cameras
Answer: B
Explanation:
Q57
A network technician is performing a wireless survey in the office and discovers a device that was not installed by the networking team. This is an example of which of following threats?
A. Bluesnarfing
B. DDoS
C. Brute force
D. Rogue AP
Answer: D
Explanation:
Q58
A technician is setting up a computer lab. Computers on the same subnet need to communicate with each other using peer to peer communication. Which of the following would the technician
MOST likely configure?
A. Hardware firewall
B. Proxy server

C. Software firewall
D. GRE tunneling
Answer: C
Explanation:

Q59
Which of the following concepts are MOST important for a company's long term health in the event of a disaster? (Select TWO).
A. Redundancy
B. Implementing acceptable use policy
C. Offsite backups
D. Uninterruptable power supplies
E. Vulnerability scanning
Answer: A,C
Explanation:

Q60
A technician needs to ensure that new systems are protected from electronic snooping of Radio Frequency emanations. Which of the following standards should be consulted?
A. DWDM
B. MIMO
C. TEMPEST
D. DOCSIS
Answer: C
Explanation:

Q61
Which of the following types of network would be set up in an office so that customers could access the Internet but not be given access to internal resources such as printers and servers?
A. Quarantine network
B. Core network
C. Guest network
D. Wireless network
Answer: C
Explanation:

Q62
A technician needs to limit the amount of broadcast traffic on a network and allow different segments to communicate with each other. Which of the following options would satisfy these requirements?
A. Add a router and enable OSPF.
B. Add a layer 3 switch and create a VLAN.

C. Add a bridge between two switches.
D. Add a firewall and implement proper ACL.
Answer: B
Explanation:
Q63
An attacker has connected to an unused VoIP phone port to gain unauthorized access to a network. This is an example of which of the following attacks?
A. Smurf attack
B. VLAN hopping
C. Bluesnarfing
D. Spear phishing
Answer: B
Explanation:
Q64
A company has decided to update their usage policy to allow employees to surf the web unrestricted from their work computers. Which of the following actions should the IT security team implement to help protect the network from attack as a result of this new policy?
A. Install host-based anti-malware software
B. Implement MAC filtering on all wireless access points
C. Add an implicit deny to the core router ACL
D. Block port 80 outbound on the company firewall
E. Require users to utilize two-factor authentication
Answer: A
Explanation:
Q65
An organization notices a large amount of malware and virus incidents at one satellite office, but hardly any at another. All users at both sites are running the same company image and receive the same group policies. Which of the following has MOST likely been implemented at the site with the fewest security issues?
A. Consent to monitoring
B. Business continuity measures
C. Vulnerability scanning
D. End-user awareness training
Answer: D
Explanation:
Q66

A wireless network technician for a local retail store is installing encrypted access points within the store for real-time inventory verification, as well as remote price checking capabilities, while employees are away from the registers. The store is in a fully occupied strip mall that has multiple neighbors allowing guest access to the wireless networks. There are a finite known number of approved handheld devices needing to access the store's wireless network. Which of the following is the BEST security method to implement on the access points?
A. Port forwarding
B. MAC filtering
C. TLS/TTLS
D. IP ACL
Answer: B
Explanation:
Q67
Ann, a network technician, was asked to remove a virus. Issues were found several levels deep within the directory structure. To ensure the virus has not infected the .mp4 files in the directory, she views one of the files and believes it contains illegal material. Which of the following forensics actions should Ann perform?
A. Erase the files created by the virus
B. Stop and escalate to the proper authorities
C. Check the remaining directories for more .mp4 files
D. Copy the information to a network drive to preserve the evidence
Answer: B
Explanation:
Q68
Which of the following describes a smurf attack?
A. Attack on a target using spoofed ICMP packets to flood it
B. Intercepting traffic intended for a target and redirecting it to another
C. Spoofed VLAN tags used to bypass authentication
D. Forging tags to bypass QoS policies in order to steal bandwidth
Answer: A
Explanation:
Q69
Which of the following technologies is designed to keep systems uptime running in the event of a disaster?
A. High availability
B. Load balancing
C. Quality of service

D. Caching engines
Answer: A
Explanation:
Q70
Packet analysis reveals multiple GET and POST requests from an internal host to a URL without any response from the server. Which of the following is the BEST explanation that describes this scenario?
A. Compromised system
B. Smurf attack
C. SQL injection attack
D. Man-in-the-middle
Answer: A
Explanation:
Q71
A network technician was tasked to respond to a compromised workstation. The technician documented the scene, took the machine offline, and left the PC under a cubicle overnight. Which of the following steps of incident handling has been incorrectly performed?
A. Document the scene
B. Forensics report
C. Evidence collection
D. Chain of custody
Answer: D
Explanation:
Q72
During a check of the security control measures of the company network assets, a network administrator is explaining the difference between the security controls at the company. Which of the following would be identified as physical security controls? (Select THREE).
A. RSA
B. Passwords
C. Man traps
D. Biometrics
E. Cipher locks
F. VLANs
G. 3DES
Answer: C,D,E
Explanation:
Q73

A technician is installing a surveillance system for a home network. The technician is unsure which ports need to be opened to allow remote access to the system. Which of the following should the technician perform?
A. Disable the network based firewall
B. Implicit deny all traffic on network
C. Configure a VLAN on Layer 2 switch
D. Add the system to the DMZ

Answer: D
Explanation:

Q74
A firewall ACL is configured as follows:
10. Deny Any Trust to Any DMZ eq to TCP port 22
11. Allow 10.200.0.0/16 to Any DMZ eq to Any
12. Allow 10.0.0.0/8 to Any DMZ eq to TCP ports 80, 443
13. Deny Any Trust to Any DMZ eq to Any

A technician notices that users in the 10.200.0.0/16 network are unable to SSH into servers in the DMZ. The company wants 10.200.0.0/16 to be able to use any protocol, but restrict the rest of the 10.0.0.0/8 subnet to web browsing only. Reordering the ACL in which of the following manners would meet the company's objectives?
A. 11, 10, 12, 13
B. 12, 10, 11, 13
C. 13, 10, 12, 11
D. 13, 12, 11, 10

Answer: A
Explanation:

Q75
A malicious user floods a switch with frames hoping to redirect traffic to the user's server. Which of the following attacks is the user MOST likely using?
A. DNS poisoning
B. ARP poisoning
C. Reflection
D. SYN attack

Answer: B
Explanation:

Q76
Which of the following is a security benefit gained from setting up a guest wireless network?
A. Optimized device bandwidth
B. Isolated corporate resources

C. Smaller ACL changes
D. Reduced password resets
Answer: B
Explanation:
Q77
A company has seen an increase in ransomware across the enterprise. Which of the following should be implemented to reduce the occurrences?
A. ARP inspection
B. Intrusion detection system
C. Web content filtering
D. Port filtering
Answer: C
Explanation:
Q78
Before logging into the company network, users are required to sign a document that is to be stored in their personnel file. This standards and policies document is usually called which of the
following?
A. SOP
B. BEP
C. AUP
D. SLA
Answer: C
Explanation:
Q79
A network technician has set up an FTP server for the company to distribute software updates for their products. Each vendor is provided with a unique username and password for security. Several vendors have discovered a virus in one of the security updates. The company tested all files before uploading them but retested the file and found the virus. Which of the following could the technician do for vendors to validate the proper security patch?
A. Use TFTP for tested and secure downloads
B. Require biometric authentication for patch updates
C. Provide an MD5 hash for each file
D. Implement a RADIUS authentication
Answer: C
Explanation:
Q80

A technician wants to securely manage several remote network devices. Which of the following should be implemented to securely manage the devices?
A. WPA2
B. IPv6
C. SNMPv3
D. RIPv2
Answer: C
Explanation:
Topic 4, Troubleshooting
Q81
A PC technician has installed a new network printer that was preconfigured with the correct static IP address, subnet mask, and default gateway. The printer was installed with a new cable and appears to have link activity, but the printer will not respond to any network communication attempts. Which of the following is MOST likely the cause of the problem?
A. Damaged cable
B. Duplex mismatch
C. Incorrect VLAN assignment
D. Speed mismatch
Answer: C
Explanation:
Q82
A network technician has detected duplicate IP addresses on the network. After testing the behavior of rogue DHCP servers, the technician believes that the issue is related to an unauthorized home router. Which of the following should the technician do NEXT in the troubleshooting methodology?
A. Document the findings and action taken.
B. Establish a plan to locate the rogue DHCP server.
C. Remove the rogue DHCP server from the network.
D. Identify the root cause of the problem.
Answer: B
Explanation:
Q83
Two weeks after installation, a network technician is now unable to log onto any of the newly installed company switches. The technician suspects that a malicious user may have changed the switches' settings before they were installed in secure areas. Which of the following is the MOST
likely way in which the malicious user gained access to the switches?

A. Via SSH using the RADIUS shared secret
B. Via HTTP using the default username and password
C. Via console using the administrator's password
D. Via SNMP using the default RO community
Answer: B
Explanation:
Q84
When a client calls and describes a problem with a computer not being able to reach the Internet, in which of the following places of the OSI model would a technician begin troubleshooting?
A. Transport layer
B. Physical layer
C. Network layer
D. Session layer
Answer: B
Explanation:
Q85
A network technician has been assigned to install an additional router on a wireless network. The router has a different SSID and frequency. All users on the new access point and the main network can ping each other and utilize the network printer, but all users on the new router cannot get to the Internet. Which of the following is the MOST likely cause of this issue?
A. The gateway is misconfigured on the new router.
B. The subnet mask is incorrect on the new router.
C. The gateway is misconfigured on the edge router.
D. The SSID is incorrect on the new router.
Answer: A
Explanation:
Q86
While troubleshooting a network outage, a technician finds a 100-meter fiber cable with a small service loop and suspects it might be the cause of the outage. Which of the following is MOST likely the issue?
A. Maximum cable length exceeded
B. Dirty connectors
C. RF interference caused by impedance mismatch
D. Bend radius exceeded
Answer: D
Explanation:
Q87

A technician is troubleshooting a wired device on the network. The technician notices that the link light on the NIC does not illuminate. After testing the device on a different RJ-45 port, the device connects successfully. Which of the following is causing this issue?
A. EMI
B. RFI
C. Cross-talk
D. Bad wiring
Answer: D
Explanation:
Q88
An organization requires a second technician to verify changes before applying them to network devices. When checking the configuration of a network device, a technician determines that a coworker has improperly configured the AS number on the device. This would result in which of the following?
A. The OSPF not-so-stubby area is misconfigured
B. Reduced wireless network coverage
C. Spanning tree ports in flooding mode
D. BGP routing issues
Answer: D
Explanation:
Q89
When configuring a new server, a technician requests that an MX record be created in DNS for the new server, but the record was not entered properly. Which of the following was MOST likely installed that required an MX record to function properly?
A. Load balancer
B. FTP server
C. Firewall DMZ
D. Mail server
Answer: D
Explanation:
Q90
A company has had several virus infections over the past few months. The infections were caused by vulnerabilities in the application versions that are being used. Which of the following should an administrator implement to prevent future outbreaks?
A. Host-based intrusion detection systems
B. Acceptable use policies

C. Incident response team
D. Patch management
Answer: D
Explanation:
Q91
A user calls the help desk and states that he was working on a spreadsheet and was unable to print it. However, his colleagues are able to print their documents to the same shared printer.
Which of the following should be the FIRST question the helpdesk asks?
A. Does the printer have toner?
B. Are there any errors on the printer display?
C. Is the user able to access any network resources?
D. Is the printer powered up?
Answer: C
Explanation:
Q92
A network technician is using a network monitoring system and notices that every device on a particular segment has lost connectivity. Which of the following should the network technician do NEXT?
A. Establish a theory of probable cause.
B. Document actions and findings.
C. Determine next steps to solve the problem.
D. Determine if anything has changed.
Answer: D
Explanation:
Q93
A technician just completed a new external website and setup access rules in the firewall. After some testing, only users outside the internal network can reach the site. The website responds to a ping from the internal network and resolves the proper public address. Which of the following could the technician do to fix this issue while causing internal users to route to the website using an internal address?
A. Configure NAT on the firewall
B. Implement a split horizon DNS
C. Place the server in the DMZ
D. Adjust the proper internal ACL
Answer: B
Explanation:
Q94

A network administrator recently installed a web proxy server at a customer's site. The following week, a system administrator replaced the DNS server overnight. The next day, customers began having issues accessing public websites. Which of the following will resolve the issue?
A. Update the DNS server with the proxy server information.
B. Implement a split horizon DNS server.
C. Reboot the web proxy and then reboot the DNS server.
D. Put the proxy server on the other side of the demarc.
Answer: A
Explanation:

Q95
While troubleshooting a connectivity issue, a network technician determines the IP address of a number of workstations is 169.254.0.0/16 and the workstations cannot access the Internet. Which of the following should the technician check to resolve the problem?
A. Default gateway address
B. Misconfigured DNS
C. DHCP server
D. NIC failure
Answer: C
Explanation:

Q96
A technician recently ran a 20-meter section of CAT6 to relocate a control station to a more central area on the production floor. Since the relocation, the helpdesk has received complaints about intermittent operation. During the troubleshooting process, the technician noticed that collisions are only observed on the switch port during production. Given this information, which of the following is the cause of the problem?
A. Distance limitation
B. Electromagnetic interference
C. Cross talk
D. Speed and duplex mismatch
Answer: B
Explanation:

Q97
A technician has finished configuring AAA on a new network device. However, the technician is unable to log into the device with LDAP credentials but is able to do so with a local user account.
Which of the following is the MOST likely reason for the problem?
A. Username is misspelled is the device configuration file

B. IDS is blocking RADIUS
C. Shared secret key is mismatched
D. Group policy has not propagated to the device
Answer: C
Explanation:
Q98
A technician is tasked with connecting a router to a DWDM. The technician connects the router to the multiplexer and confirms that there is a good signal level. However, the interface on the router will not come up. Which of the following is the MOST likely cause?
A. The wrong wavelength was demuxed from the multiplexer.
B. The SFP in the multiplexer is malfunctioning.
C. There is a dirty connector on the fiber optic cable.
D. The fiber optic cable is bent in the management tray.
Answer: A
Explanation:
Q99
A network technician is performing a tracert command to troubleshoot a website-related issue. The following output is received for each hop in the tracert:
1 * * * Request timed out.
2 * * * Request timed out.
3 * * * Request timed out.
The technician would like to see the results of the tracert command. Which of the following will allow the technician to perform tracert on external sites but not allow outsiders to discover information from inside the network?
A. Enable split horizon to allow internal tracert commands to pass through the firewall
B. Enable IGMP messages out and block IGMP messages into the network
C. Configure the firewall to allow echo reply in and echo request out of the network
D. Install a backdoor to access the router to allow tracert messages to pass through
Answer: C
Explanation:
Topic 5, Industry Standards, Practices, and Network Theory
Q100
Which of the following describes an area containing a rack that is used to connect customer equipment to a service provider?
A. 110 block

B. MDF
C. DSU
D. CSU
Answer: B
Explanation:
Q101
A network technician must utilize multimode fiber to uplink a new networking device. Which of the following Ethernet standards could the technician utilize? (Select TWO).
A. 1000Base-LR
B. 1000Base-SR
C. 1000Base-T
D. 10GBase-LR
E. 10GBase-SR
F. 10GBase-T
Answer: B,E
Explanation:
Q102
A network administrator is using a packet analyzer to determine an issue on the local LAN. Two separate computers are showing an error message on the screen and are unable to communicate with other computers in the same lab. The network administrator looks at the following output:
SRC MAC SRC IP DST MAC DST IP
00:1D:1F:AB:10:7D 192.168.1.10:2000 15:BE:9F:AB:10:1D 192.168.1.14:1200
05:DD:1F:AB:10:27 192.168.1.10:1000 22:C7:2F:AB:10:A2 192.168.1.15:1300
Given that all the computers in the lab are directly connected to the same switch, and are not using any virtualization technology, at which of the following layers of the OSI model is the problem occurring?
A. Network
B. Application
C. Data link
D. Transport
Answer: A
Explanation:
Q103
Which of the following requires the network administrator to schedule a maintenance window?
A. When a company-wide email notification must be sent.

B. A minor release upgrade of a production router.
C. When the network administrator's laptop must be rebooted.
D. A major release upgrade of a core switch in a test lab.
Answer: B
Explanation:
Q104
Which of the following is true about the main difference between a web session that uses port 80 and one that uses port 443?
A. Port 80 web sessions often use application-level encryption, while port 443 sessions often use
transport-level encryption.
B. Port 80 web session cannot use encryption, while port 443 sessions are encrypted using web
certificates.
C. Port 80 web sessions can use web application proxies, while port 443 sessions cannot traverse
web application proxies.
D. Port 80 web sessions are prone to man-in-the-middle attacks, while port 443 sessions are
immune from man-in-the-middle attacks.
Answer: A
Explanation:
Q105
The management team wants to set up a wireless network in their office but all of their phones operate at the 2.4 GHz frequency. They need a wireless network that would be able to operate at a higher frequency than their phones. Which of following standards should be used?
A. 802.11a
B. 802.11b
C. 802.11g
D. 802.1x
Answer: A
Explanation:
Q106
Which of the following will negotiate standoff timers to allow multiple devices to communicate on congested network segments?
A. CSMA/CD
B. OSPF
C. DOCSIS
D. BGP

Answer: A
Explanation:
Q107
A service provider is unable to maintain connectivity to several remote sites at predetermined speeds. The service provider could be in violation of the:
A. MLA.
B. SLA.
C. SOW.
D. MOU.
Answer: B
Explanation:
Q108
A network administrator has created a virtual machine in the cloud. The technician would like to connect to the server remotely using RDP. Which of the following default ports needs to be opened?
A. 445
B. 3389
C. 5004
D. 5060
Answer: B
Explanation:
Q109
Which of the following is an example of an IPv4 address?
A. 192:168:1:55
B. 192.168.1.254
C. 00:AB:FA:B1:07:34
D. ::1
Answer: B
Explanation:
Q110
Which of the following does a network technician need to implement if a change is unsuccessful within the approved maintenance window?
A. Configuration procedures
B. Stakeholder notification
C. Impact analysis
D. Rollback procedure
Answer: D
Explanation:
Q111
Which of the following is the main difference between TCP and UDP?

A. TCP data flows in two directions, while UDP data flows from server to client.
B. The TCP header implements flags, while the UDP header does not.
C. The TCP header implements checksum, while the UDP header does not.
D. TCP connections can be secured by stateful firewalls, while UDP connections cannot.
Answer: B
Explanation:
Q112
Which of the following PDUs is used by a connectionless protocol?
A. Frames
B. Segments
C. Streams
D. Datagram
Answer: D
Explanation:
Q113
When troubleshooting a network problem, browsing through the log of a switch, it is discovered that multiple frames contain errors. In which of the following layers does the problem reside?
(Select TWO).
A. Layer 2
B. Layer 3
C. Layer 5
D. Transport layer
E. Data link
F. Physical layer
Answer: A,E
Explanation:
Q114
A network technician is attempting to locate a switch connected to the fourth floor west side of the building. Which of the following will allow quick identification of the switch, when looking at a logical diagram?
A. Building layout
B. Patch panel labeling
C. Packet sniffing
D. Naming conventions
Answer: D
Explanation:

Q115
In an engineering office, all plotters are configured via static IP. Which of the following best practices will alleviate many issues if equipment moves are required? (Select TWO).
A. Rack monitoring
B. Device placement
C. Wall plate labeling
D. Room numbering
E. Patch panel labeling
Answer: C,E
Explanation:

Q116
Which of the following devices implements CSMA/CA virtually through the RTS/CTS protocols?
A. Firewall
B. Router
C. 802.11 AP
D. Switch
Answer: C
Explanation:

Q117
A user with a 802.11n WLAN card is connected to a SOHO network and is only able to connect at 11 Mbps with full signal strength. Which of the following standards is implemented on the network?
A. 802.11a
B. 802.11ac
C. 802.11b
D. 802.11g
Answer: C
Explanation:

Q118
A network technician is attempting to connect a new host to existing manufacturing equipment on an Ethernet network. The technician is having issues trying to establish communication between the old equipment and the new host. The technician checks the cabling for breaks and finds that the CAT3 cable in use is in perfect condition. Which of the following should the technician check to ensure the new host will connect?
A. Confirm the new host is using 10GBaseSR due to the manufacturing environment
B. Confirm the new host is compatible with 10BaseT Ethernet

C. Confirm the existing 10Base2 equipment is using the proper frame type
D. Confirm that CSMA/CD is disabled on the Ethernet network
Answer: B
Explanation:
Q119
A customer has engaged a company to improve the availability of all of the customer's services and applications, enabling the customer to minimize downtime to a few hours per quarter. Which of the following will document the scope of the activities the company will provide to the customer, including the intended outcomes?
A. MLA
B. MOU
C. SOW
D. SLA
Answer: C
Explanation:
Q120
A network technician has just installed a TFTP server on the administrative segment of the network to store router and switch configurations. After a transfer attempt to the server is made, the process errors out. Which of the following is a cause of the error?
A. Only FTP can be used to copy configurations from switches
B. Anonymous users were not used to log into the TFTP server
C. An incorrect password was used and the account is now locked
D. Port 69 is blocked on a router between the network segments
Answer: D
Explanation:
Q121
An organization is moving to a new datacenter. During the move, several technicians raise concerns about a system that could potentially remove oxygen from the server room and result in suffocation. Which of the following systems are they MOST likely discussing?
A. Fire suppression
B. Mantraps at the entry
C. HVAC
D. UPS and battery backups
Answer: A
Explanation:
Topic 6, Mixed Set
Q122

A technician, Joe, needs to troubleshoot a recently installed NIC. He decides to ping the local loopback address. Which of the following is a valid IPv4 loopback address?
A. 10.0.0.1
B. 127.0.0.1
C. 172.16.1.1
D. 192.168.1.1
Answer: B
Explanation:
Q123
A host has been assigned the address 169.254.0.1. This is an example of which of the following address types?
A. APIPA
B. MAC
C. Static
D. Public
Answer: A
Explanation:
Q124
An F-connector is used on which of the following types of cabling?
A. CAT3
B. Single mode fiber
C. CAT5
D. RG6
Answer: D
Explanation:
Q125
After repairing a computer infected with malware, a technician determines that the web browser fails to go to the proper address for some sites. Which of the following should be checked?
A. Server host file
B. Subnet mask
C. Local hosts file
D. Duplex settings
Answer: C
Explanation:
Q126
A company wants to make sure that users are required to authenticate prior to being allowed on the network. Which of the following is the BEST way to accomplish this?

A. 802.1x
B. 802.1p
C. Single sign-on
D. Kerberos
Answer: A
Explanation:
Q127
A technician, Joe, has been tasked with assigning two IP addresses to WAN interfaces on connected routers. In order to conserve address space, which of the following subnet masks should Joe use for this subnet?
A. /24
B. /32
C. /28
D. /29
E. /30
Answer: E
Explanation:
Q128
Joe, a network technician, is setting up a DHCP server on a LAN segment. Which of the following options should Joe configure in the DHCP scope, in order to allow hosts on that LAN segment using dynamic IP addresses, to be able to access the Internet and internal company servers?
(Select THREE).
A. Default gateway
B. Subnet mask
C. Reservations
D. TFTP server
E. Lease expiration time of 1 day
F. DNS servers
G. Bootp
Answer: A,B,F
Explanation:
Q129
An administrator only has telnet access to a remote workstation. Which of the following utilities will identify if the workstation uses DHCP?
A. tracert
B. ping
C. dig
D. ipconfig
E. netstat

Answer: D
Explanation:
Q130
Which of the following protocols uses label-switching routers and label-edge routers to forward traffic?
A. BGP
B. OSPF
C. IS-IS
D. MPLS
Answer: D
Explanation:
Q131
A network technician has received a help desk ticket indicating that after the new wireless access point was installed, all of the media department's devices are experiencing sporadic wireless connectivity. All other departments are connecting just fine and the settings on the new access point were copied from the baseline. Which of the following is a reason why the media department
is not connecting?
A. Wrong SSID
B. Rogue access point
C. Placement
D. Channel mismatch
Answer: C
Explanation:
Q132
A user connects to a wireless network at the office and is able to access unfamiliar SMB shares and printers. Which of the following has happened to the user?
A. The user is connected using the wrong channel.
B. The user is connected to the wrong SSID.
C. The user is experiencing an EMI issue.
D. The user is connected to the wrong RADIUS server.
Answer: B
Explanation:
Q133
Which of the following network devices use ACLs to prevent unauthorized access into company systems?
A. IDS
B. Firewall

C. Content filter
D. Load balancer
Answer: B
Explanation:

Q134
Ann, a user, is experiencing an issue with her wireless device. While in the conference area, the wireless signal is steady and strong. However, at her desk the signal is consistently dropping, yet the device indicates a strong signal. Which of the following is the MOST likely cause of the issue?
A. Signal-to-noise ratio
B. AP configuration
C. Incorrect SSID
D. Bounce
Answer: D
Explanation:

Q135
A network engineer is troubleshooting an issue with a computer that is unable to connect to the Internet. The network engineer analyzes the following output from a command line utility:
Network Destination Netmask Gateway Interface
192.168.1.0 255.255.255.0 192.168.1.254 eth0
192.168.1.10 255.255.255.255 192.168.1.10 eth0
127.0.0.1 255.0.0.0 On-Link lo
127.0.0.0 255.0.0.0 On-Link lo
255.255.255.255 255.255.255.255 102.168.1.10 eth0
Which of the following is the reason for the computer issue, given the above output?
A. Wrong default gateway netmask
B. Incorrect default gateway address
C. Default gateway on the wrong interface
D. Missing default gateway
Answer: D
Explanation:

Q136
A network engineer is dispatched to an employee office to troubleshoot an issue with the employee's laptop. The employee is unable to connect to local and remote resources. The network engineer flips the laptop's wireless switch on to resolve the issue. At which of the following layers of the OSI model was the issue resolved?
A. Layer 1

B. Layer 2
C. Layer 3
D. Layer 4
E. Layer 7
Answer: A
Explanation:
Q137
A network technician has received comments from several users that cannot reach a particular website. Which of the following commands would provide the BEST information about the path taken across the network to this website?
A. ping
B. netstat
C. telnet
D. tracert
Answer: D
Explanation:
Q138
A network technician has detected a personal computer that has been physically connected to the corporate network. Which of the following commands would the network technician use to locate this unauthorized computer and determine the interface it is connected to?
A. nbtstat -a
B. show mac address-table
C. show interface status
D. show ip access-list
E. nslookup hostname
Answer: B
Explanation:
Q139
A network technician is troubleshooting a problem at a remote site. It has been determined that the connection from router A to router B is down. The technician at the remote site re-terminates the CAT5 cable that connects the two routers as a straight through cable. The cable is then tested and is plugged into the correct interface. Which of the following would be the result of this action?
A. The normal amount of errors and the connection problem has been resolved.
B. The interface status will indicate that the port is administratively down.
C. The traffic will flow, but with excessive errors.

D. The interface status will show line protocol down.
Answer: D
Explanation:
Q140
After connecting a workstation directly to a small business firewall, a network administrator is trying to manage it via HTTPS without losing its stored configuration. The only two pieces of information that the network administrator knows about the firewall are the management interface MAC address, which is 01:4a:d1:fa:b1:0e, and the administrator's password. Which of the following will allow the administrator to log onto the firewall via HTTPS if the management's IP address is unknown and the administrator's workstation IP address is 192.168.0.10/23?
A. Use the reset button on the back of the firewall to restore it to its factory default, and then log
onto
B. Run the following command on the administrator's workstation: arp -s 192.168.1.200
01:4a:d1:fa:b1:0e
C. Use an SNMP tool to query the firewall properties and determine the correct management IP
address
D. Use a crossover cable to connect to the console port and reconfigure the firewall management
IP to 192.168.0.1
Answer: B
Explanation:
Q141
Which of the following connection types is used to terminate DS3 connections in a telecommunications facility?
A. 66 block
B. BNC
C. F-connector
D. RJ-11
Answer: B
Explanation:
Q142
A desktop computer is connected to the network and receives an APIPA address but is unable to reach the VLAN gateway of 10.10.100.254. Other PCs in the VLAN subnet are able to reach the Internet. Which of the following is MOST likely the source of the problem?

A. 802.1q is not configured on the switch port
B. APIPA has been misconfigured on the VLAN
C. Bad SFP in the PC's 10/100 NIC
D. OS updates have not been installed
Answer: A
Explanation:
Q143
A technician is setting up a new network and wants to create redundant paths through the network. Which of the following should be implemented to prevent performance degradation?
A. Port mirroring
B. Spanning tree
C. ARP inspection
D. VLAN
Answer: B
Explanation:
Q144
A network technician is utilizing a network protocol analyzer to troubleshoot issues that a user has been experiencing when uploading work to the internal FTP server. Which of the following default port numbers should the technician set the analyzer to highlight when creating a report? (Select TWO).
A. 20
B. 21
C. 22
D. 23
E. 67
F. 68
G. 69
Answer: A,B
Explanation:
Q145
A network engineer needs to set up a topology that will not fail if there is an outage on a single piece of the topology. However, the computers need to wait to talk on the network to avoid congestions. Which of the following topologies would the engineer implement?
A. Star
B. Bus
C. Ring
D. Mesh

Answer: C
Explanation:
Q146
A technician needs to secure web traffic for a new e-commerce website. Which of the following will secure traffic between a web browser and a website?
A. SSL
B. DNSSEC
C. WPA2
D. MTU
Answer: A
Explanation:
Q147
A network technician is assisting the company with developing a new business continuity plan. Which of the following would be an appropriate suggestion to add to the plan?
A. Build redundant links between core devices
B. Physically secure all network equipment
C. Maintain up-to-date configuration backups
D. Perform reoccurring vulnerability scans
Answer: A
Explanation:
Q148
A company has changed ISPs for their office and ordered a new 250 Mbps symmetrical Internet connection. As a result, they have been given a new IP range. The ISP has assigned the company 10.10.150.16 /28. The company gateway router has the following interface configuration facing the ISP:
Interface A:
IP address: 10.10.150.16
Subnet mask: 255.255.255.240
Default gateway: 10.10.150.32
Speed: 1000 Mbps
Duplex: Auto
State: No Shutdown
None of the workstations at the company are able to access the Internet. Which of the following are the reasons? (Select TWO).
A. There is a duplex mismatch between the router and ISP.
B. The router interface is turned off.
C. The interface is set to the incorrect speed.

D. The router is configured with the incorrect subnet mask.
E. The router interface is configured with the incorrect IP address.
F. The default gateway is configured incorrectly.
Answer: E,F
Explanation:
Q149
The ability to make access decisions based on an examination of Windows registry settings, antivirus software, and AD membership status is an example of which of the following NAC features?
A. Quarantine network
B. Persistent agents
C. Posture assessment
D. Non-persistent agents
Answer: C
Explanation:
Q150
A technician is troubleshooting a client's connection to a wireless network. The client is asked to run a "getinfo" command to list information about the existing condition.
myClient$ wificard --getinfo
agrCtlRSSI: -72
agrExtRSSI: 0
state: running
op mode: station
lastTxRate: 178
MaxRate: 300
802.11 auth: open
link auth: wpa2-psk
BSSID: 0F:33:AE:F1:02:0A
SSID: CafeWireless
Channel: 149,1
Given this output, which of the following has the technician learned about the wireless network?
(Select TWO).
A. The WAP is using RC4 encryption
B. The WAP is using 802.11a
C. The WAP is using AES encryption
D. The WAP is using the 2.4GHz channel
E. The WAP is using the 5GHz channel
F. The WAP is using 802.11g

Answer: C,E
Explanation:
Q151
A technician has prolonged contact with a thermal compound. Which of the following resources should be consulted?
A. HCL
B. MSDS
C. SLA
D. HVAC
Answer: B
Explanation:
Q152
CORRECT TEXT
Wireless network users recently began experiencing speed and performance issues after access point 2 (AP2) was replaced due to faulty hardware. The original network was installed according to a consultant's specifications and has always worked without a problem.
You, a network technician, have been tasked with evaluating the situation and resolving the issues to improve both performance and connectivity.
Refer to the following diagram and perform any NECESSARY changes to the wireless and wired infrastructure by adjusting devices.
Note: Adjust the LEAST number of devices needed to fix the issue, our blue icons in the image in this book is not clickable. But you will want to go thru the motions using a separate sheet of paper for your answers, and when you feel you have completed your choices move to the next.

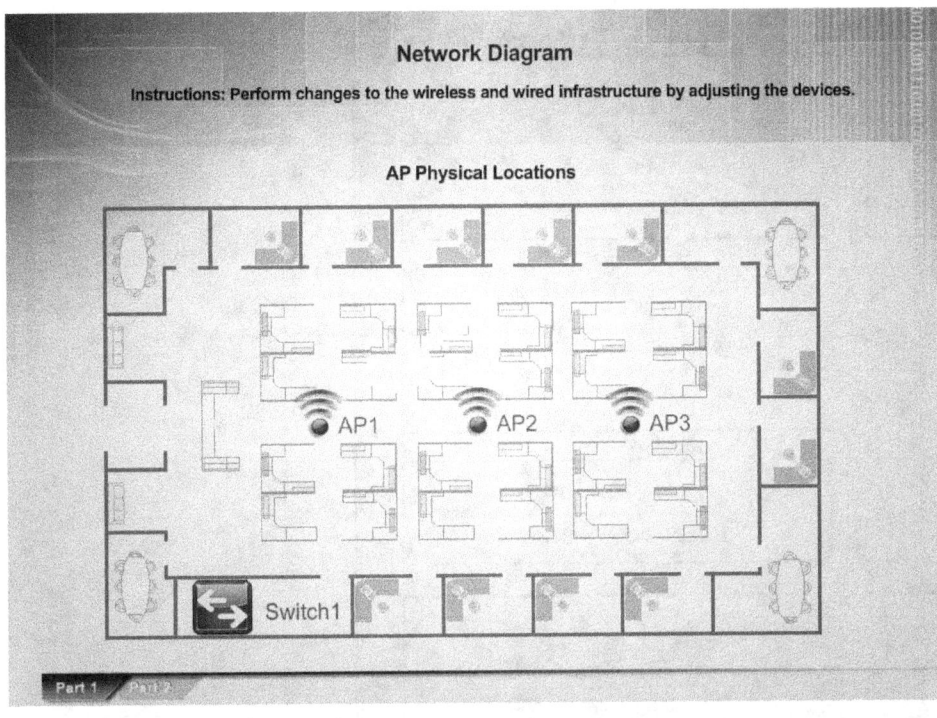
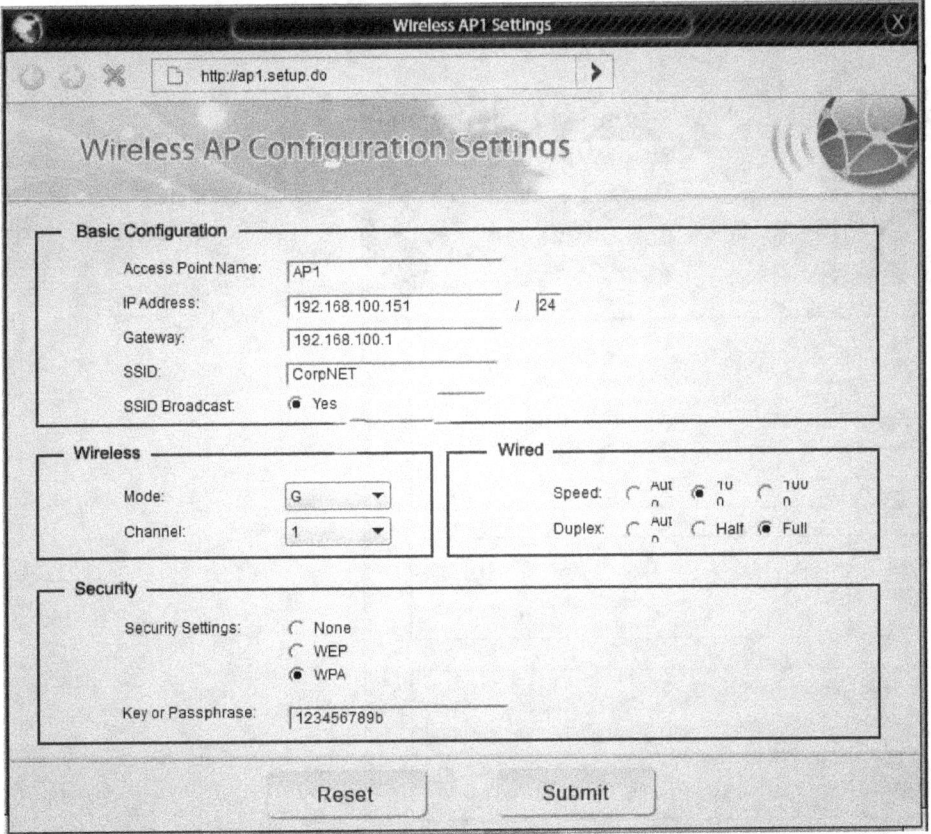

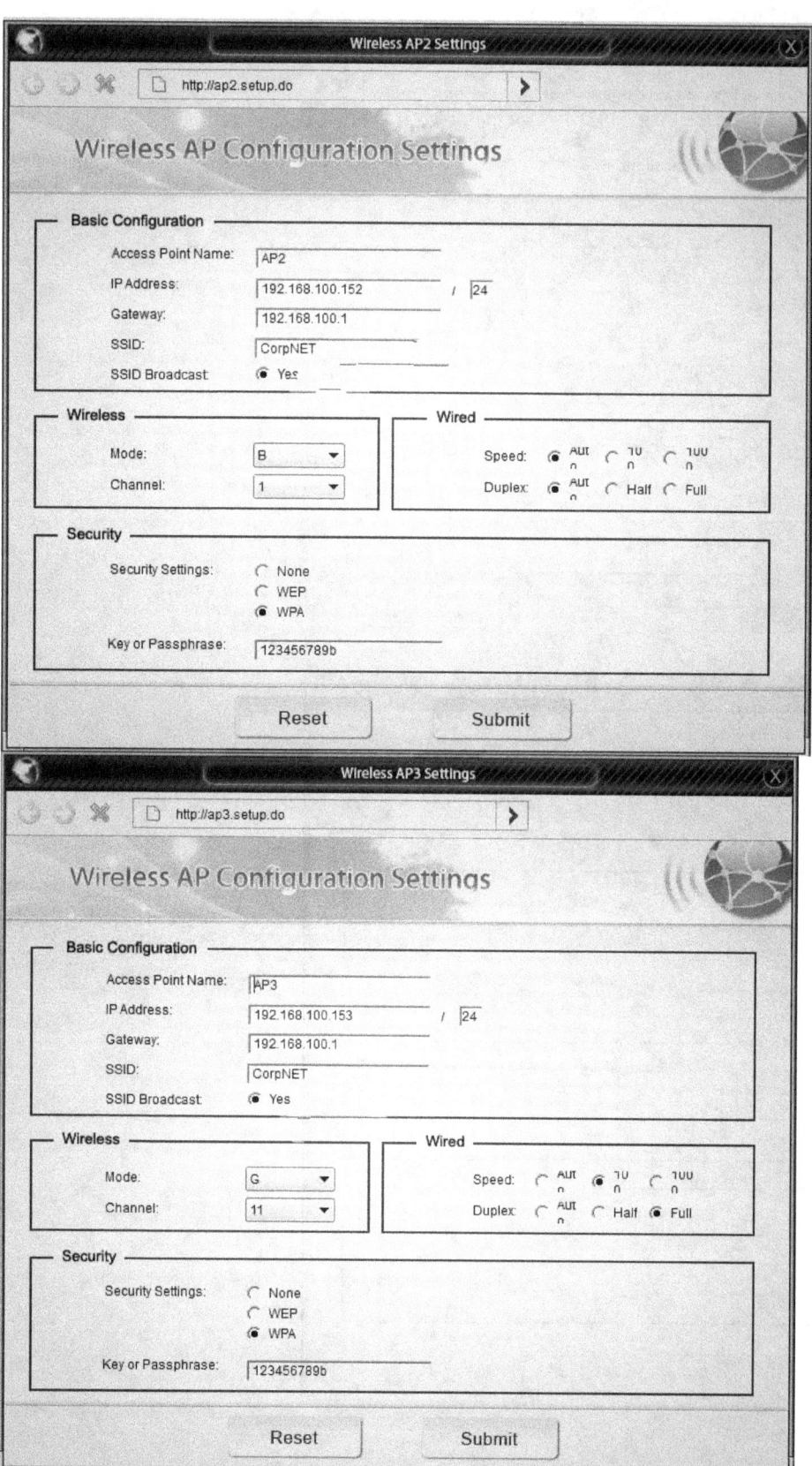

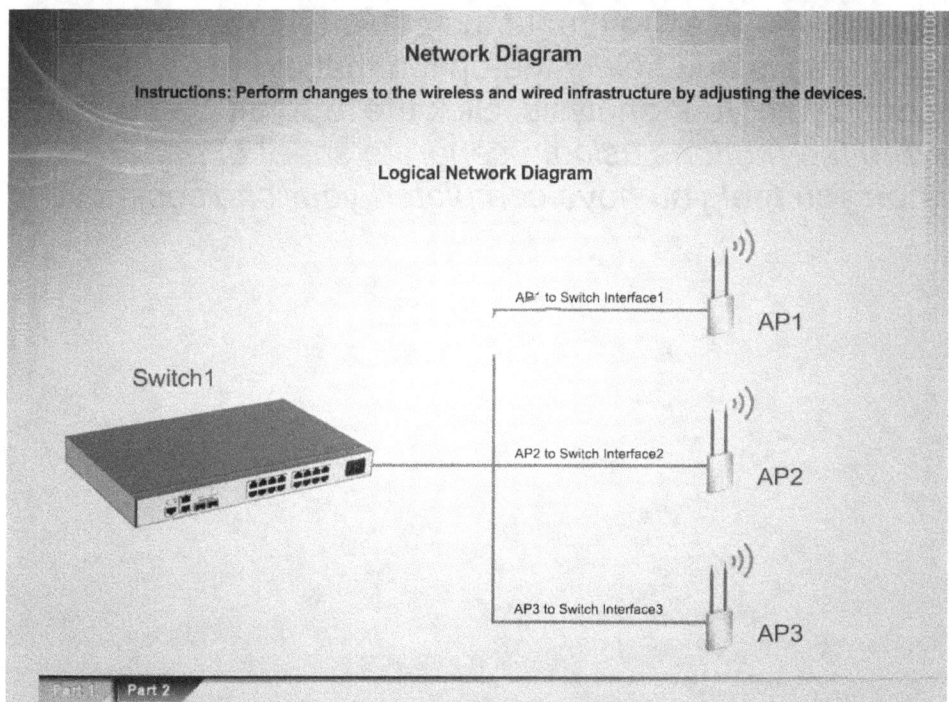

Answer:

Answer: -Change the speed and duplex settings on AP2 only to 100 and full.
-Change the mode to G on AP2
-Change the channel to 6 on AP2
Explanation:
Since we know that the network was running perfectly before replacing AP2 we should start by looking at this new device that was used to replace the old one. Here we see that the other AP's have hard coded the speed and duplex settings to 100/full, while AP2 is set to auto/auto.
Also, the other AP's have been configured to use 802.11G, while AP2 is using 802.11B. Finally the channel that AP2 is using overlaps with AP1 which can cause problems. Channels 1, 6, and 11 are spaced far enough apart that they don't overlap. On a non-MIMO setup (i.e. 802.11 a,
b, or g) you should always try to use channel 1, 6, or 11. Since AP1 is using 1, and AP3 is using 11, AP2 should be using 6.
Q153
CORRECT TEXT
You have been tasked with testing a CAT5e cable. A summary of the test results can be found on the screen.
Step 1: Select the tool that was used to create the cable test results.
Step 2: Interpret the test results and select the option that explains the results. After you are done with your analysis, click the 'Submit Cable Test Analysis' button. (*go thru the motions using a separate sheet of paper for your answers, and when you feel you have completed your choices move to the next.*)

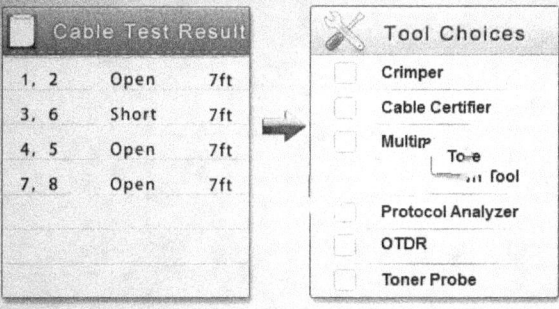

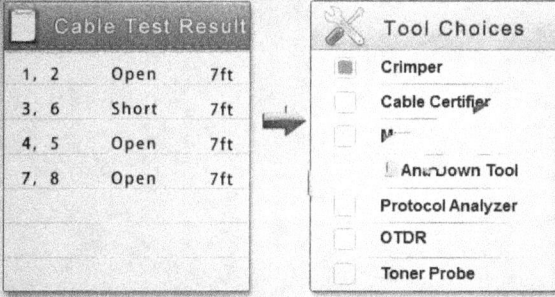

Cable Test

Step 1: Select the tool that was used to create the cable test results.

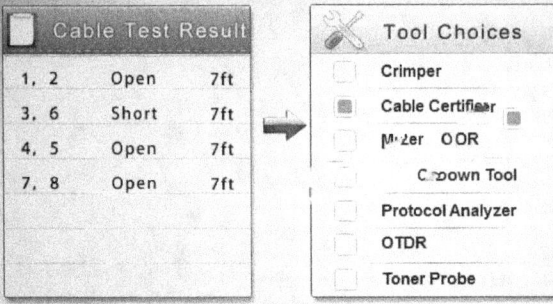

Step 2: Interpret the test results and select the option that explains the results.
After you are done with your analysis, click the 'Submit Cable Test Analysis' button.

○ Correctly crimped cable
○ Incorrectly crimped cable

[Submit Cable Test Analysis]

Cable Test

Step 1: Select the tool that was used to create the cable test results.

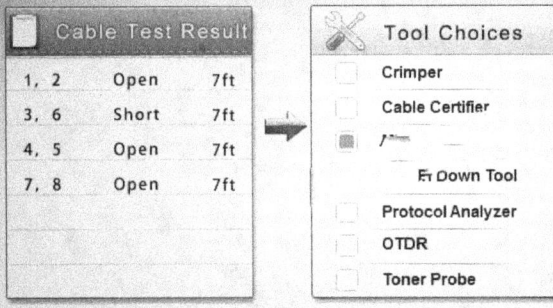

Step 2: Interpret the test results and select the option that explains the results.
After you are done with your analysis, click the 'Submit Cable Test Analysis' button.

○ Correct voltage on the cable
○ Incorrect voltage on the cable

[Submit Cable Test Analysis]

Cable Test

Step 1: Select the tool that was used to create the cable test results.

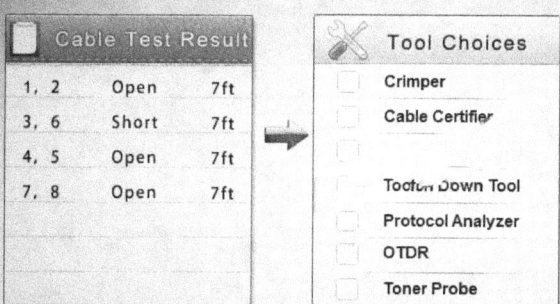

Step 2: Interpret the test results and select the option that explains the results.
After you are done with your analysis, click the 'Submit Cable Test Analysis' button.

- ○ Correctly punched cable
- ○ Incorrectly punched cable

[Submit Cable Test Analysis]

Cable Test

Step 1: Select the tool that was used to create the cable test results.

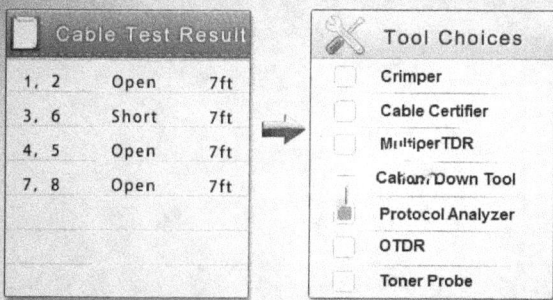

Step 2: Interpret the test results and select the option that explains the results.
After you are done with your analysis, click the 'Submit Cable Test Analysis' button.

- ○ Correct captured packets
- ○ Incorrect captured packets

[Submit Cable Test Analysis]

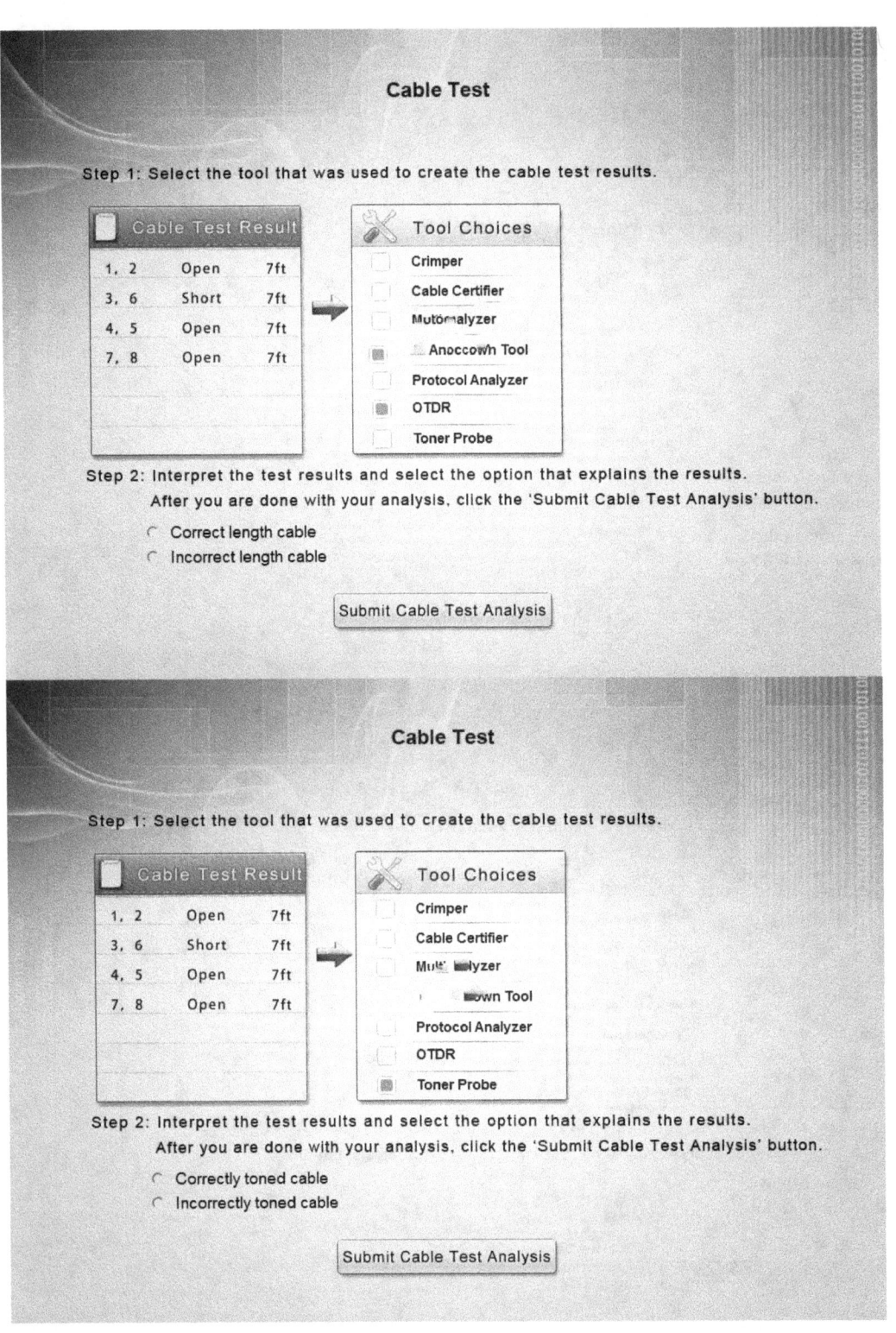

Answer:
Answer: Solution is pending.
Q154
CORRECT TEXT

Alter recent changes to the pictured network, several users are unable to access the servers. Only PC1, PC2, PC3, and PC4 are clickable and will give you access to the command prompt and the adapter configuration tabs.

Instructions: Verify the settings by using the command prompt, after making any system changes.

Next, restore connectivity by making the appropriate changes to the infrastructure. When you have completed these steps, select the Done button to submit. (*go thru the motions using a separate sheet of paper for your answers, and when you feel you have completed your choices move to the next.*)

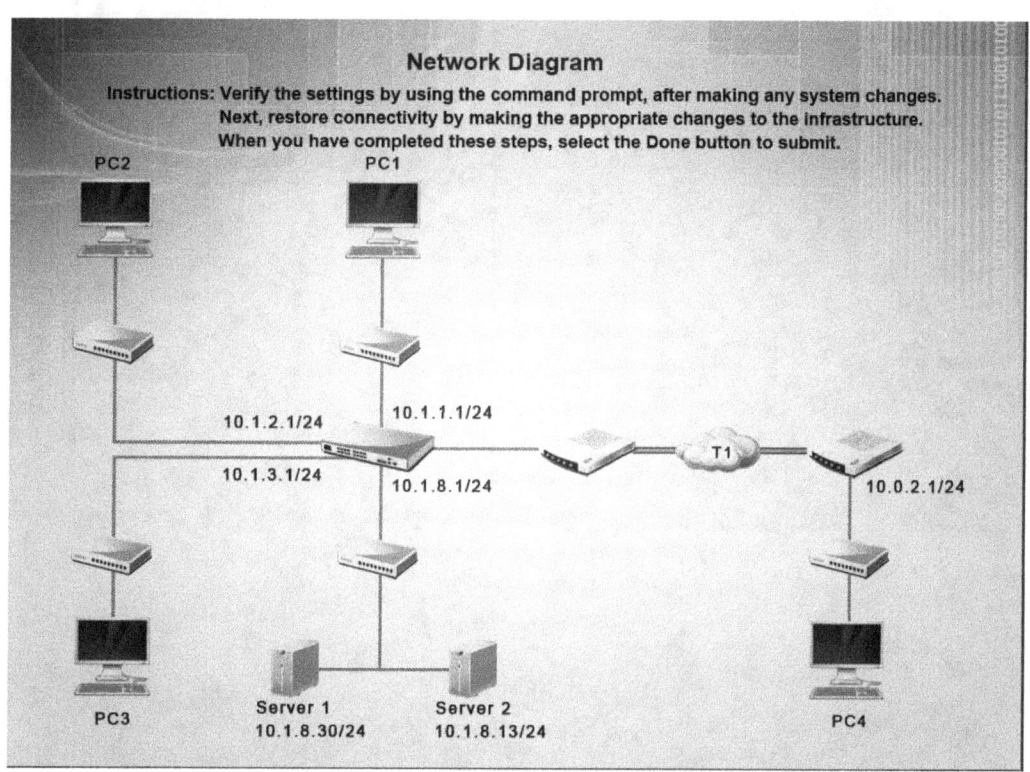

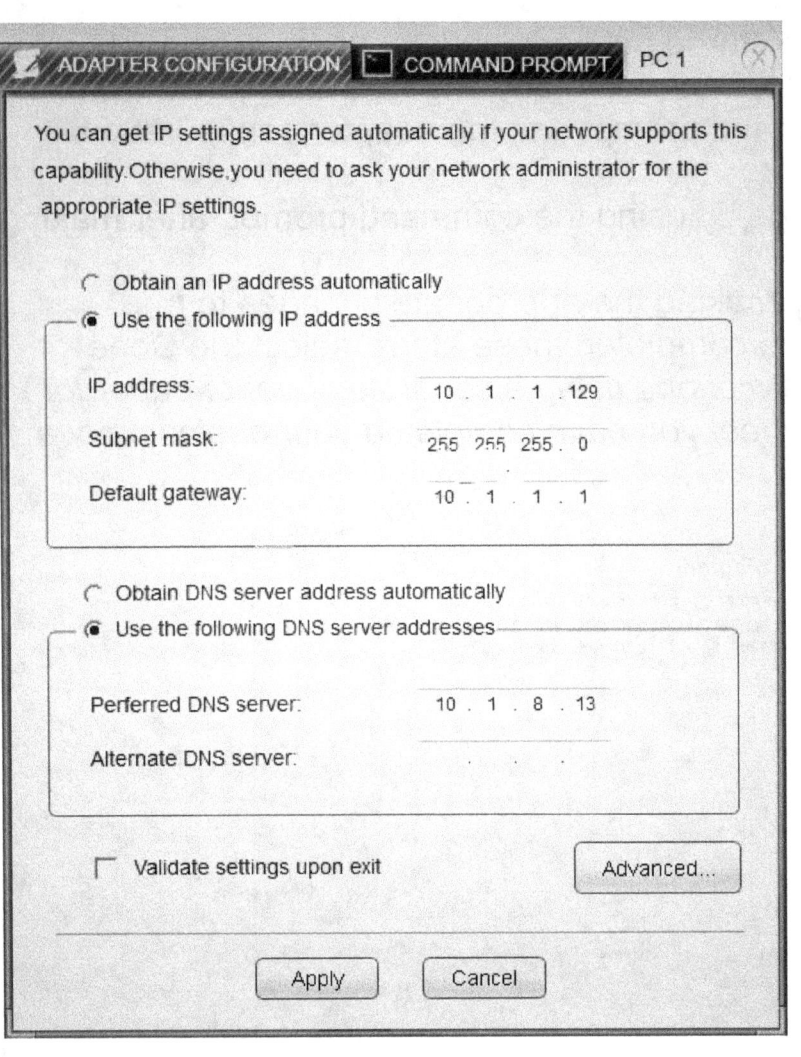

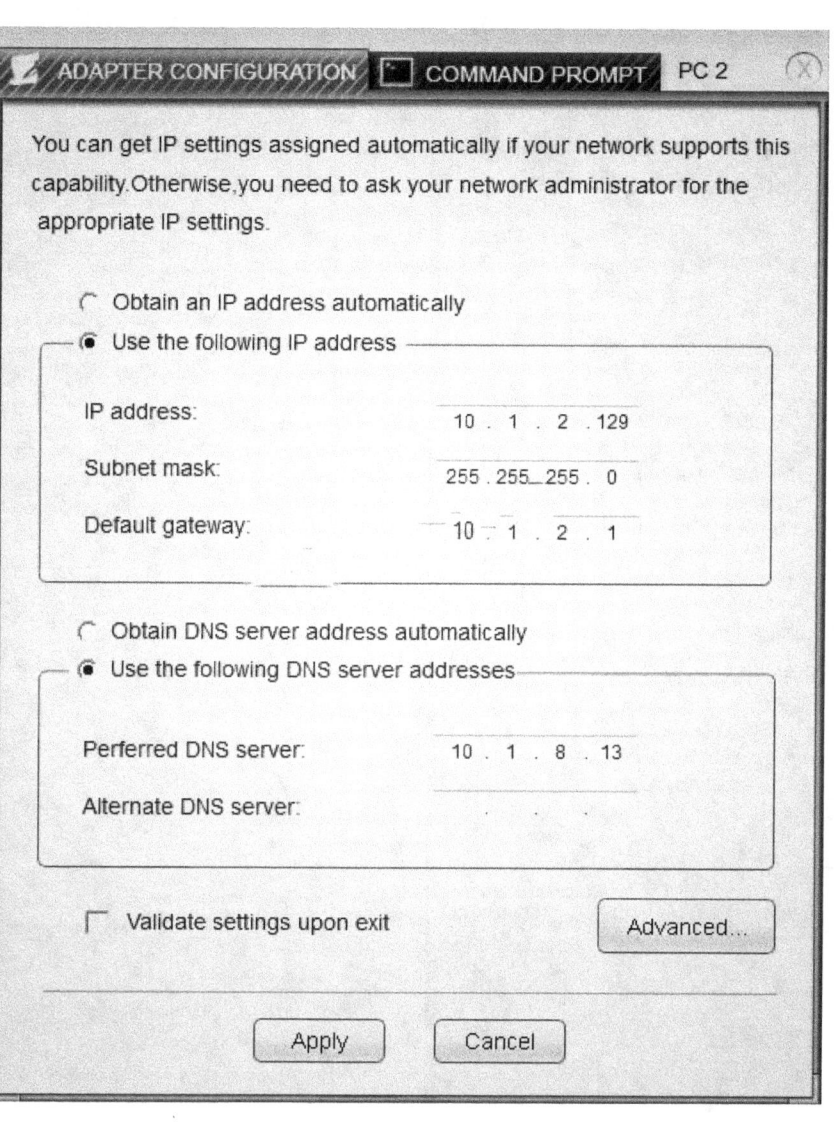

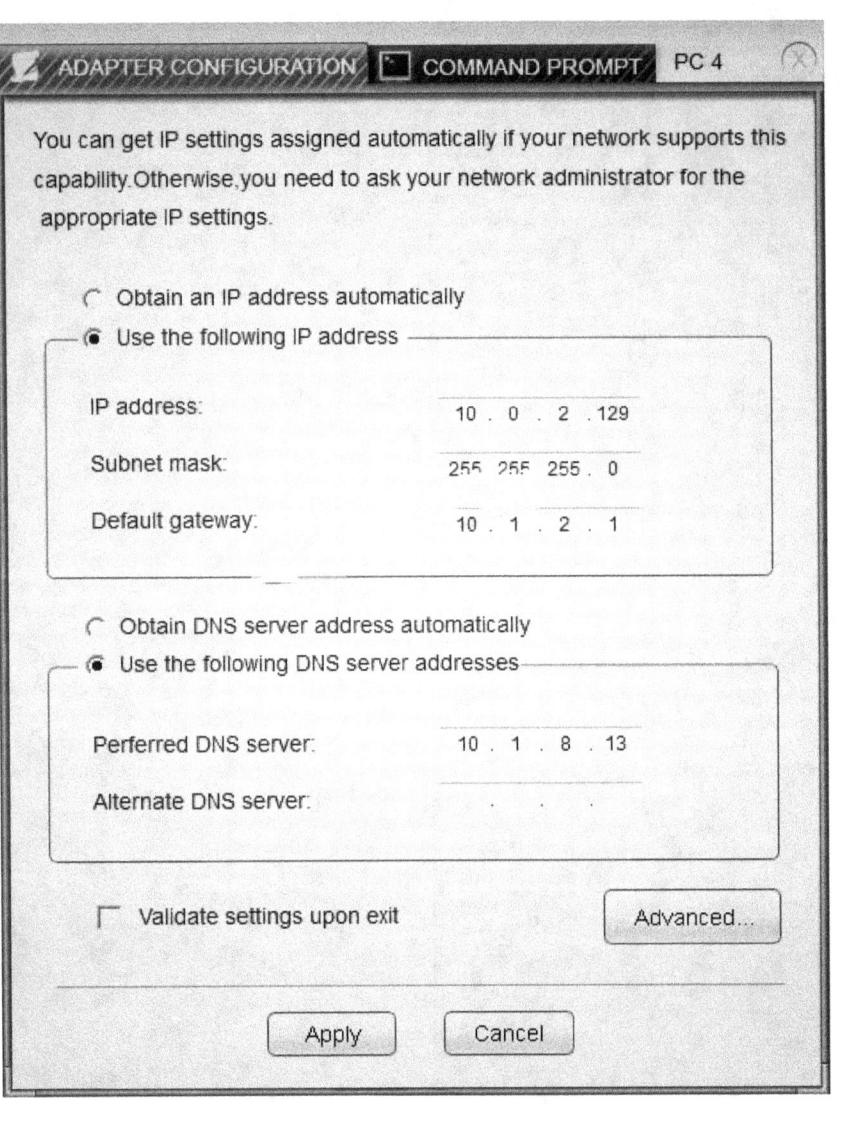

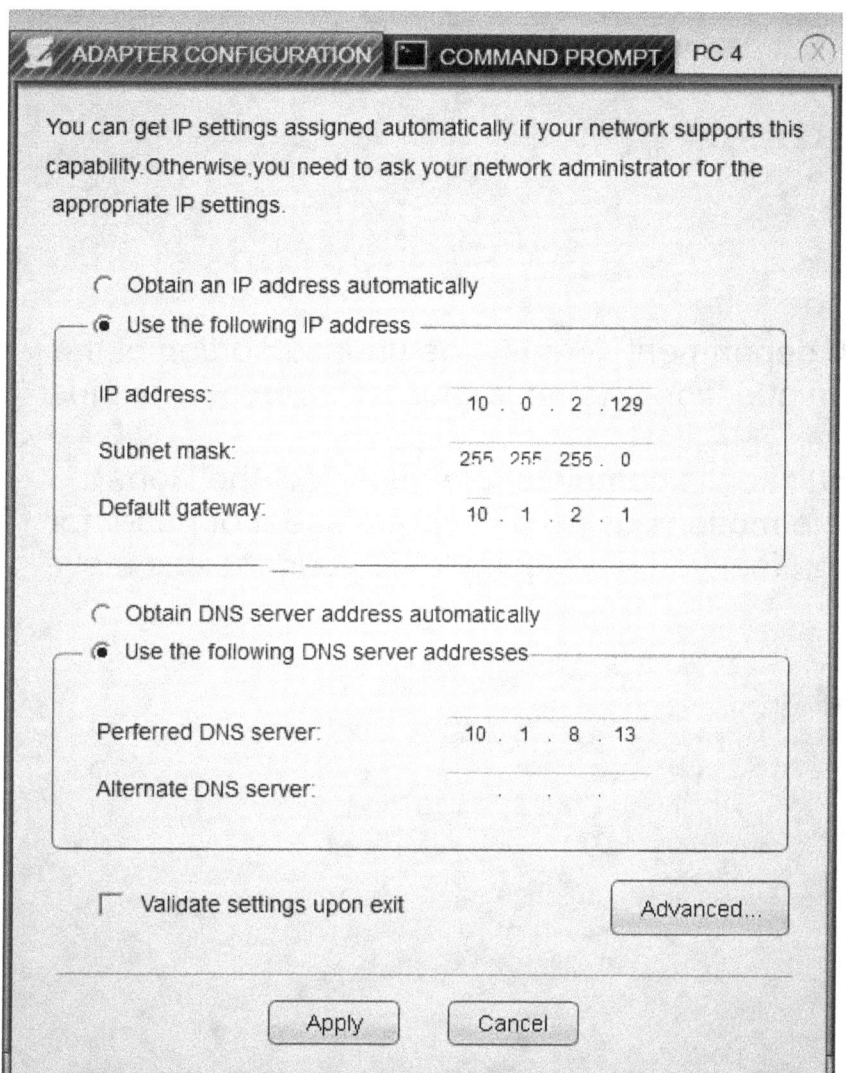

Answer:
Answer: On PC3, change the subnet mask to 255.255.255.0. When it is set to 255.255.255.128, then the PC with a .129 address will not be on the same subnet as the default gateway which is .1 On PC4, change the default gateway to 10.0.2.1. It has been incorrectly set as 10.1.2.1.
Q155
HOTSPOT
Corporate headquarters provided your office a portion of their class B subnet to use at a new office location. Allocate the minimum number of addresses (using CIDR notation) needed to
accommodate each department.

Range Given: 172.30.232.0/24

- Sales   57 devices
- HR   23 devices
- IT   12 devices
- Finance   32 devices
- Marketing   9 devices

Alter accommodating each department, identify the unused portion of the subnet by responding to the question on the graphic. All drop downs must be filled.
Instructions: When the simulation is complete, please select the Done button to submit. (go thru the motions using a separate sheet of paper for your answers, and when you feel you have completed your choices move to the next.)

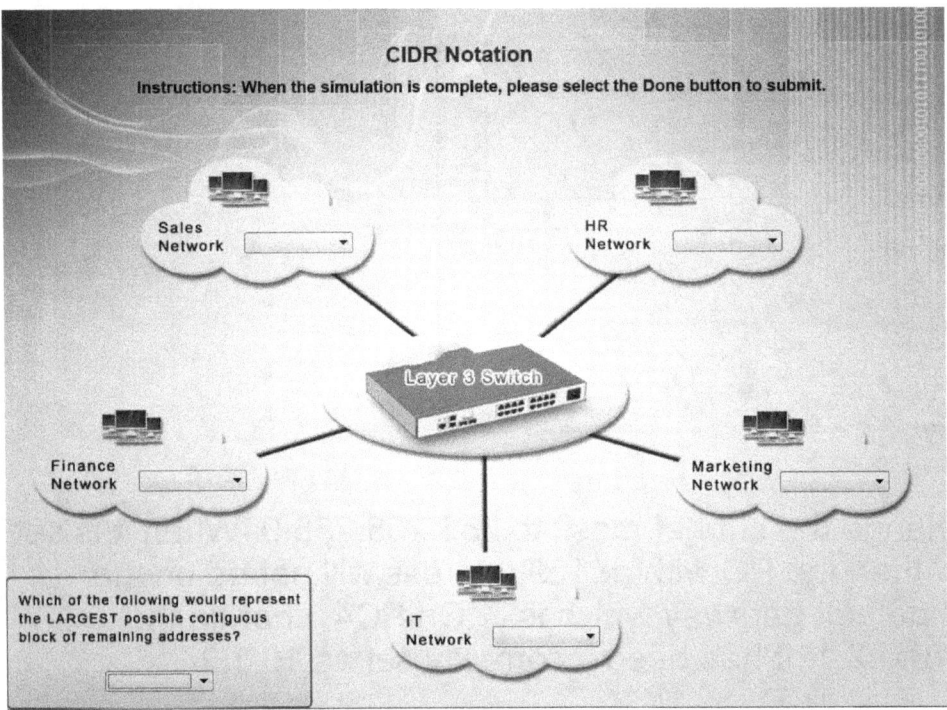

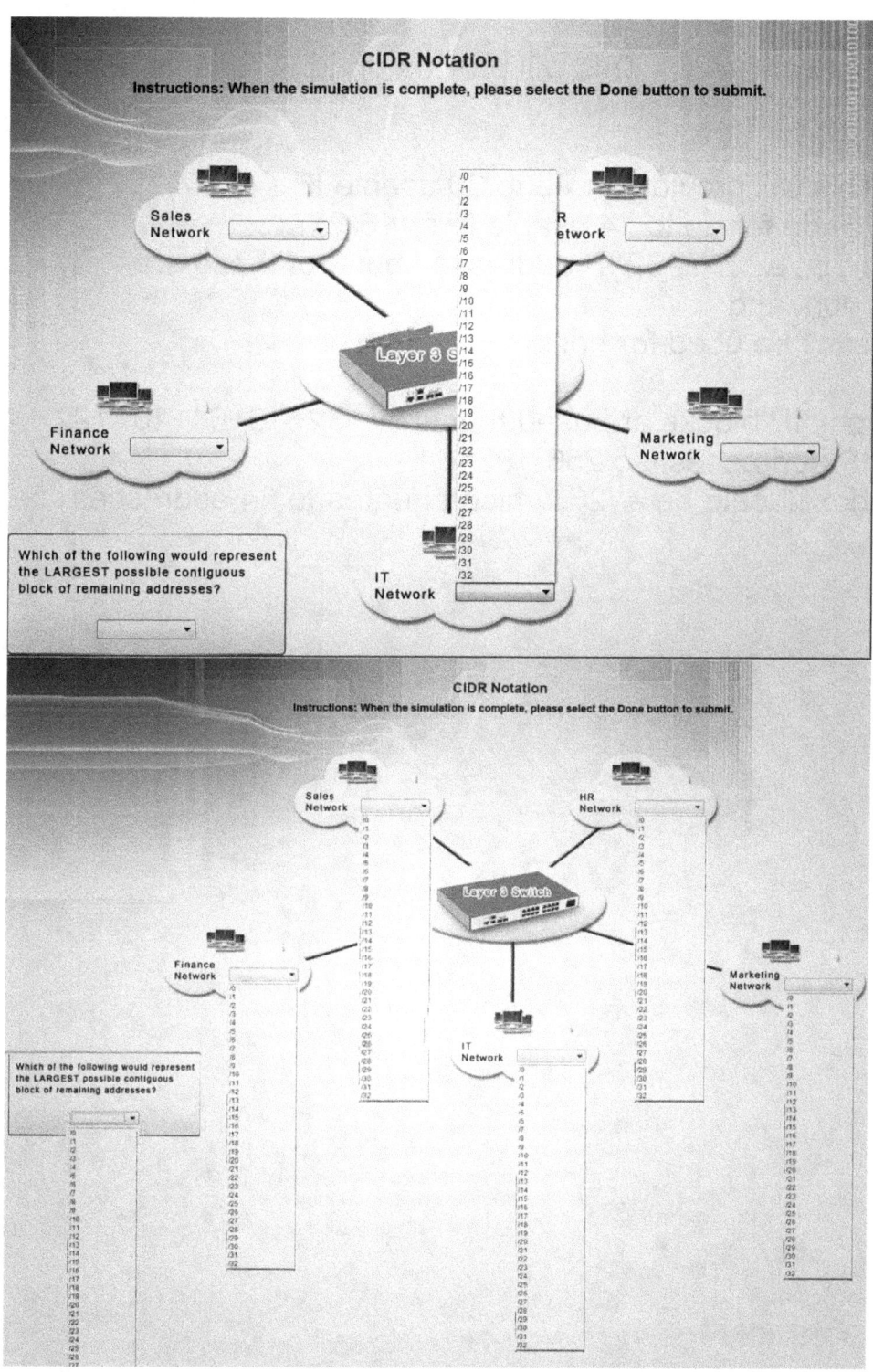

All Networks have the range form /0 to/32
Answer:

Explanation: Sales network - /26 - This will provide up to 62 usable IP addresses (64-2 for
subnet and broadcast IP)
HR network - /27 - This will provide for up to 30 usable IP's (32-2)
IT - /28 - This will provide for up to 14 usable IP's (16-2)
Finance - /26 - Note that a /27 is 32 IP addresses but 2 of those are reserved for the network and
broadcast IP's and can't be used for hosts.
Marketing - /28
If we add up how many IP blocks are used that is 64+32+16+64+16=192.
A /24 contains 256 IP addresses, so 256-192=64.
So the last unused box should be a /26, which equates to 64 addresses

THE END.